Maths at Work

Maths at the Train Station

Tracey Steffora

Raintree is an imprint of Capstone Global Library Limited, a company incorporated in England and Wales having its registered office at 7 Pilgrim Street, London, EC4V 6LB – Registered company number: 6695582

To contact Raintree please phone 0845 6044371, fax + 44 (0) 1865 312263, or email myorders@ raintreepublishers.co.uk. Customers from outside the UK please telephone +44 1865 312262.

Text © Capstone Global Library Limited 2013
First published in hardback in 2013
The moral rights of the proprietor have been asserted.

Edited by Dan Nunn and Abby Colich
Designed by Victoria Allen
Picture research by Tracy Cummins
Production control by Victoria Fitzgerald
Printed and bound in China by Leo Paper Products Ltd

ISBN 978 1 406 25074 9
16 15 14 13 12
10 9 8 7 6 5 4 3 2 1

British Library Cataloguing in Publication Data
Steffora, Tracey.
Maths at the train station. – (Maths at work)
510-dc23
A full catalogue record for this book is available from the British Library.

Acknowledgements
We would like to thank the following for permission to reproduce photographs: Alamy: pp. 5 (© Patrick Eden), 9 (© David Mark); Corbis: p. 11 (© Construction Photography); Getty Images: pp. 12 (AFP Photo Patrick Kovarik), 13 (Eric Hood); Newscom: p. 6 (ZUMA Press); Photoshot: p. 7 (© Rafael Ben-Ari/Chameleons Eye); Shutterstock: pp. 4 (John Leung), 8 (Ungor), 10 (auremar), 14 (Frances L Fruit), 16 (ARENA Creative), 18 (joyfull), 19 (apiguide), 20 (Don Long), 21 (PaulPaladin), 22a (Ungor), 22b (ARENA Creative), 22c (apiguide); Superstock: p. 15 (© imagebroker.net).

Front cover photograph of a Tokyo train station reproduced with permission from Alamy (© Picture Contact BV).

Back cover photograph a young man driving a tram reproduced with permission from Shutterstock (auremar).

Every effort has been made to contact copyright holders of any material reproduced in this book. Any omissions will be rectified in subsequent printings if notice is given to the publisher.

Contents

Maths at the train station

People work at the train station.

People use maths at the train station.

Counting

cashier

The cashier counts money.

conductor

The conductor counts tickets.

platform

The platforms have numbers.

How many platforms can you count? (answer on page 22)

Measuring

train driver

The train driver drives the train.

The train driver measures how far to the next stop.

how fast

The train driver measures how fast the train is going.

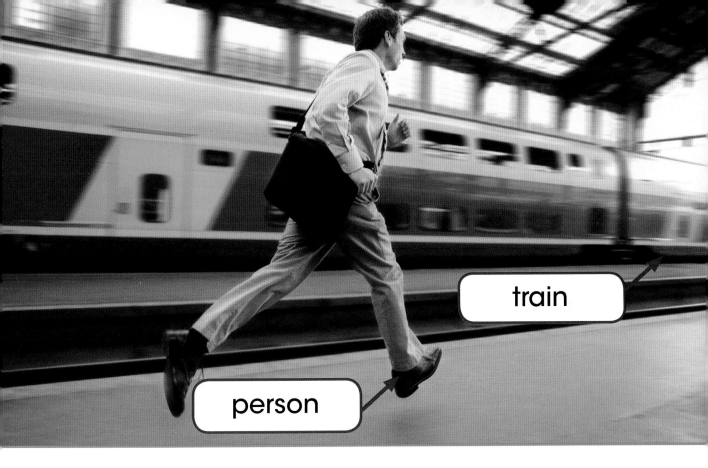

train

person

Which is faster? The person or the train? (answer on page 22)

Time

The conductor knows what time
a train leaves.

The conductor knows what time
a train arrives.

TRAIN INFO

Time	Number	Train	To	From		
			WASHINGTON	BOSTON	ON TIME	
			GRAND CENTRAL	NEW HAVEN	ON TIME	14
1:18	2159	ACELA EXPRESS	RICHMOND	BOSTON	ON TIME	10
1:57	1559	METRO-NORTH	BOSTON	WASHINGTON	ON TIME	
2:11	93	REGIONAL	GRAND CENTRAL	NEW HAVEN	ON TIME	
2:38	172	REGIONAL	OLD SAYBROOK	NEW HAVEN	ON TIME	
2:57	1563	METRO-NORTH	WASHINGTON	BOSTON		
3:00	1622	SHORE LINE EAST				
3:18	2163	ACELA EXPRESS				

PASSENGERS PLEASE WATCH YOUR BELONGINGS / SECURITY

WILL REMOVE ANY UNATTENDED BAGS

timetable

The timetable shows what time
each train leaves.

Birmingham	9:00 a.m.

What time does the train to Bristol leave? (answer on page 22)

17

Shapes

These workers build the tracks.

straight line

Some tracks are straight.

curved line

Some tracks are curved.

Are these tracks straight or curved?

(answer on page 22)

Answers

page 9: There are two platforms.

page 13: The train is faster.

page 17: The train leaves at 8.00 a.m. (a.m. means in the morning).

page 21: The tracks are curved.

Picture glossary

platform raised area where people get on and off trains

timetable list that shows the time things happen

track metal rails on which trains travel

Index

Notes for parents and teachers

Maths is a way that we make sense of the world around us. For the young child, this includes recognizing similarities and differences, classifying objects, recognizing shapes and patterns, developing number sense, and using simple measurement skills.

Before reading

Connect with what children know

Allow children to share any experience they have travelling on trains. Talk about the different jobs people have at the train station and on board trains.

After reading

Build upon children's curiosity and desire to explore

- If possible, have a set of toy train tracks available in both straight and curved shapes. Discuss the difference between "straight" and "curved" and why straight tracks are used in real life (along a city street, pulling into a station, etc.) and curved tracks are sometimes needed (to go around a mountain, etc.). Ask them to sort the tracks into two piles. Extend by showing how curved tracks can make a circle and how inserting straight tracks changes this shape.